CONTENTS

Did you know?

Discover some interesting facts about Norse myths.

WHO'S WHO?

Find out more about some of the main characters in Norse myths.

MYTH LINKS

Learn about similar characters or stories from other cultures.

THE NORSE WORLD

The people who lived in Scandinavia from the 8th to 12th centuries were called the Norsemen, or sometimes Vikings or Danes. At first, the Norsemen mostly lived by farming but they were also great raiders and explorers. From about AD 800, they began to sail to other parts of Europe, raiding monasteries and towns for loot. Soon, they also began to settle in some of the lands they visited.

They were spurred on by a lack of good, fertile farmland at home. The Norsemen were brave and ruthless warriors, spreading terror wherever they went. However, they were also skilled craftsmen, and talented poets and storytellers.

MYTHS AND LEGENDS

Myths and legends are traditional stories. They are not based on historical fact but tell stories about gods and goddesses, supernatural beings, and events, such as the creation of the world and what happens after death. Since ancient times people have been telling these stories to help make sense of their lives and the world around them.

The Norsemen had a rich collection of myths, mostly describing the behaviour and adventures of the gods. At first, the myths were passed on by word of mouth through storytellers, called skalds. They were often composed as poems, which may have helped the skalds to remember them. Later on, they were written down (see below).

Did you know?

The Norse myths were first written down in Iceland in the 13th century. The two main sources are called the Eddas, which retell the myths in poem and prose. The *Prose Edda* was written by the Icelandic scholar and politician, Snorri Sturluson, who lived from 1179 to 1241.

MYTHS

NORSE
MYTHS AND
LEGENDS

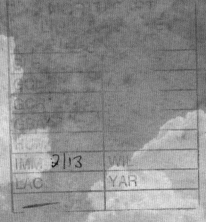

Anita Ganeri

Raintree

Raintree is an imprint of Capstone Global Library Limited, a company incorporated in England and Wales having its registered office at 7 Pilgrim Street, London, EC4V 6LB – Registered company number: 6695582

To contact Raintree please phone 0845 6044371, fax + 44 (0) 1865 312263, or email myorders@raintreepublishers.co.uk. Customers from outside the UK please telephone +44 1865 312262.

Text © Capstone Global Library Limited 2013
First published in paperback in 2013
The moral rights of the proprietor have been asserted.

Edited by Nancy Dickmann, Adam Miller, and Claire Throp
Designed by Jo Hinton-Malivoire
Original illustrations © Capstone Global Library Ltd 2013
Illustrations by Xöul
Picture research by Hannah Taylor
Production by Victoria Fitzgerald
Originated by Capstone Global Library Ltd
Printed and bound in China by Leo Paper Products Ltd

ISBN 978 1 406 24995 8
16 15 14 13 12
10 9 8 7 6 5 4 3 2 1

British Library Cataloguing in Publication Data
Ganeri, Anita
Norse myths and legends. – (All about myths)
398.2'09368-dc23
A full catalogue record for this book is available from the British Library.

Acknowledgements
We would like to thank the following for permission to reproduce photographs: Alamy Images pp. 7 (© Sindre Ellingsen), 21 (© Ivy Close Images), 23 (© imagebroker), 22 (© The Art Gallery Collection), 40 (© Mary Evans Picture Library), 41 (© Ivy Close Images); Corbis pp. 8 (Atli Mar Hafsteinsson/Nordicphotos), 15 (Felix Zaska), 17 (Werner Forman), 20 (Christophe Boisvieux), 37 (Werner Forman); Getty Images pp. 13, 14 (DEA/G. DAGLI ORTI/De Agostini), 36 (Jeffry Weymier); Shutterstock pp. 4 (©Arunas Gabalis), 6 (© Ozerov Alexander), 27 (© David Persson); SuperStock pp. 5 (David Lomax), 9 (Newberry Library), 12 (Clover), 28 (Douglas Houghton); The Art Archive pp. 29 (Richard Wagner Museum Bayreuth/ Alfredo Dagli Orti), 35 (Cavalry Museum Pinerolo/Dagli Orti); The Bridgeman Art Library pp. 16 (© Nationalmuseum, Stockholm, Sweden), 26 (Arni Magnusson Institute, Reykjavik, Iceland), 30 (Private Collection), 31 (Private Collection/ Photo © The Fine Art Society, London, UK), 34 (Private Collection).

Background images: Shutterstock (©3drenderings), (©Amy Johansson), (©StockCube), (©J. Helgason), (©Dm_Cherry), (©Dm_Cherry), (©Andreas Gradin), (©Algol), (©Triff).

Cover photograph of a stone Viking statue reproduced with permission of Getty Images (Duncan Walker). Cover graphic: Shutterstock (© Martin Capek).

The publishers would like to thank Roderick Dale of the Centre for the Study of the Viking Age at the University of Nottingham for his invaluable assistance in the production of this book.

Note: for how to pronounce Norse names, see pages 42–43.

The Norsemen sailed in ships like this one.

5

THE NINE WORLDS

In Norse mythology, the universe was made up of the Nine Worlds. These were arranged in three levels, one above the other. On the highest level were Asgard and Vanaheim, the worlds of the Norse gods and goddesses. Here, they lived in magnificent halls, roofed in gold and silver.

WHO'S WHO?

One god, Heimdall, had such good hearing that he could hear a sound as quiet as grass growing. He also had superb eyesight, was immensely strong, and needed very little sleep. Because of these special qualities, he was appointed guardian of Bifrost. He will blow his horn to warn the gods of the giants' approach at the start of Ragnarok (see page 41).

A rainbow bridge, called Bifrost, linked Asgard, the world of the gods, to Midgard, the world of humans.

MYTH LINKS

In Hindu mythology, the universe is arranged in circles around Mount Meru, the sacred mountain. The mountain is said to be made from gold and to be located in the Himalayas, the highest peaks on Earth. At the top, are the cities of the gods. Further down are the continents and oceans. Below these are the underworlds and hells.

HUMAN WORLD

Below the worlds of the gods was Midgard, the world of humans. It was surrounded by an ocean so vast that no human could cross it. In it lurked the dreadful serpent, Jormungand, whose body circled around Earth. This middle level of the universe was also home to the giants and dwarves (see pages 30–31). Midgard was linked to Asgard by Bifrost, the rainbow bridge.

■ Midgard was the world of humans where the Norsemen lived in settlements like this one.

LAND OF THE DEAD

At the lowest level of the universe was Niflheim, the land of ice, and Muspell, the land of fire. Muspell was the home of the fire giants. Niflheim was the Land of the Dead, a gloomy place of snow and cold which lay in permanent darkness. The Norsemen believed that those who did not die a brave or heroic death ended up in Niflheim. Niflheim was ruled over by the goddess Hel, a terrifying figure whose body and face were as black as a rotting corpse on one side but normal on the other. Niflheim's gates were guarded by Garm, a huge, ferocious dog with a blood-stained chest.

WORLD TREE

At the centre of the Norse universe was a gigantic ash tree, called Yggdrasill. It was so vast that all of the Nine Worlds were shaded by its branches or held in place by its three massive roots.

One root spread to Asgard where it was tended by three women, called the Norns, who decided people's destinies. Another root reached into Jotunheim, realm of the frost giants. The third root stretched into Niflheim where a dragon, Nidhogg, gnawed at it constantly.

Did you know?

Icy Niflheim and fiery Muspell may have been inspired by the landscape of Iceland where the Norse myths were written down (see page 4). Located far to the north, large parts of the country are covered in ice sheets and glaciers. There are also many active volcanoes, spurting out red-hot lava from cracks in the ground.

How the world began

Long ago, before the world existed, there was a place of ice and snow, called Niflheim, in the north. In the south was a place of fire and flames, called Muspell. Between the two lay a vast and gaping emptiness – this was Ginnungagap.

Eleven raging rivers flowed out of Niflheim and streamed into Ginnungagap, where they froze solid among the frost and wind. When the rivers of ice neared the glowing heat of Muspell, they began to melt and drip. From these icy drops, two creatures were formed. One was an evil frost giant, called Ymir. When he slept, he began to sweat, and from his sweat more frost giants were made. The other creature was a giant cow, called Audumla. Ymir lived by drinking Audumla's milk while Audumla licked the ice for nourishment.

One day, as Audumla was licking the ice, the shape of a giant began to emerge. The giant was Buri, who in time had a son, named Bor. Bor married Bestla, a frost giantess, and they had three sons: the gods Odin, Vili, and Ve. Odin and his brothers hated Ymir and his cruel band of frost giants and, eventually, they killed him. Ymir's blood flowed out in torrents, drowning all the frost giants except two, who escaped in a hollowed-out tree trunk.

Odin, Vili, and Ve hoisted Ymir's body on to their shoulders, dragged it to the middle of Ginnungagap, and used it to create the world. They shaped Earth from Ymir's flesh and made the mountains from his bones. His teeth became the rocks and stones, and his blood filled the rivers and seas. His skull became the sky and his brains were tossed into the air as clouds. Finally, Odin, Vili, and Ve took some of the sparks and embers from Muspell and scattered them in the sky as the Sun, Moon, and stars.

THE FIRST HUMANS

One day, while the Norse gods Odin, Vili, and Ve were walking by the sea, they came across two tree trunks, washed up on the shore. One was an ash tree and the other was an elm. The gods decided to bring them back to life but in a new form, as the first humans. Odin breathed life into the trees, while Vili gave them sharp wits and feelings. Ve gave them the gifts of sight, hearing, and speech. The ash tree became the first man, Ask; the elm tree became the first woman, Embla. The gods gave them their own world, Midgard, to live in.

Did you know?

Ash and elm were important trees for the Norsemen, who sometimes used their wood for building ships. Ships were also made from oak, which was sacred to Odin.

SUN AND MOON

Another Norse myth tells how the Sun and Moon appeared in the sky. In Midgard, a man had two children who were so beautiful that he named them Moon and Sun, after the Moon and Sun that the gods had created. The gods were angry and snatched his children away. They placed them in the sky to drive and guide the chariots of the Sun and Moon.

MYTH LINKS

In Mayan mythology, the gods tried three times to make the first humans. First, they tried making people from mud but they collapsed in a heap. Next, they used wood but the people were stiff and could not feel or think. Finally, they tried maize flour and this worked perfectly.

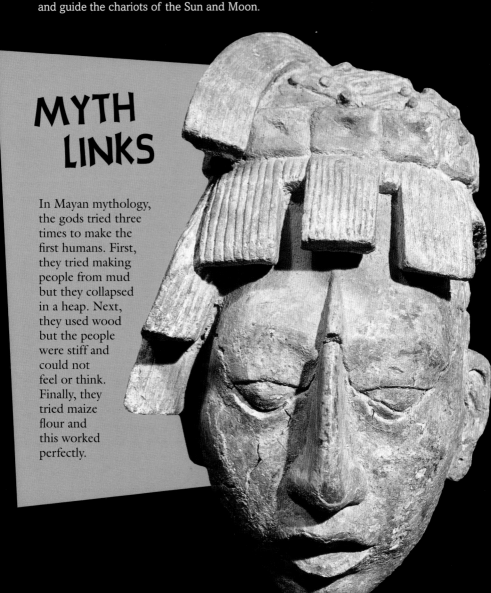

GODS AND GODDESSES

The Norsemen worshipped many different gods and goddesses who affected every aspect of their world and daily lives. In many ways, the gods were very like human beings. They fell in love, got married, fought each other, and had many extraordinary adventures. Unlike the gods in many other cultures, though, the Norse gods were not immortal. This meant that their lives were often in danger and they could be killed. Most of them were doomed to die at Ragnarok, the end of the world (see page 41).

This picture stone from Sweden shows Odin, the king of the gods, receiving warriors in his hall in Valhalla.

Did you know?

Very little is known about how the Norsemen worshipped. The only surviving accounts were written down about 200 years after their religion had died out and they had converted to Christianity. We do know that Norse chiefs may have acted as priests and that horses were sometimes sacrificed to the gods.

WAR BETWEEN THE GODS

The two main groups of Norse gods were the Aesir and the Vanir. They reflected two important sides of Viking society: war and farming. The Aesir were warrior gods and included Odin, king of the gods, and Thor, god of thunder. The Vanir were fertility gods who ruled over the sea and Earth. Norse myths tell of a long war between the two, during which the great wall surrounding Asgard (the home of the Aesir) was demolished. After the war, which ended in a truce, the wall was rebuilt by a giant and his magical horse.

■ Norse warriors and farmers worshipped the gods that were most important to them in their daily lives.

THE THUNDER GOD

Thor, god of thunder, was Odin's eldest son. He had wild
red hair and beard, and a fiery temper. Everything Thor
did was on a grand scale – feasting, fighting, and drinking.
Despite this, he was god of law and order, protecting both
gods and humans against evil.

Did you know?

The 2011 film *Thor* tells the story of a comic book superhero based on the Norse god. Exiled from Asgard, Thor lands on Earth and is captured by scientists. From Earth, he must find a way of stopping Loki, who plans to steal his rightful place as king of the gods.

WHO'S WHO?

Thor was married to Sif, the harvest goddess, who was famous for her long, golden hair. One day, the trickster god, Loki, cut off Sif's hair. The world went dark and the crops died. Threatened with death by Thor, Loki asked the dwarves for help. They spun a magic length of gold for Sif that grew like real hair and replaced her own.

Mjollnir was a fearsome weapon which always hit its target and returned to Thor's hand.

TREASURES OF THE GODS

The Norse myths tell of certain objects that gave the gods magical powers, such as a ship that always had the wind behind it when it sailed. Thor had a belt which doubled his already massive strength.

Thor's greatest treasure was Mjollnir, a hammer made for him by the dwarves. When Thor flung down his hammer, lightning flashed across the sky.

The theft of Thor's hammer

One morning, Thor woke up to find that Mjollnir had gone. Bursting with rage, he searched Asgard but it was nowhere to be found. The other gods grew worried. Without Mjollnir, it would not be long before the giants stormed the walls of Asgard and brought the gods' world crashing down.

Loki offered to help find Thor's hammer. He borrowed the goddess Freyja's magic falcon skin that allowed the wearer to fly, and set off for Jotunheim, the land of the giants. There he found Thrym. Thrym admitted that he had stolen Mjollnir and hidden the hammer deep under ground. "You can have it back," he chuckled. "If you give me Freyja as my bride."

Freyja refused. Luckily, Heimdall, the watchman, came up with a cunning plan. "Dress Thor up as a bride and send him to Thrym instead," he said, 'Loki can go as his bridesmaid! By the time Thrym realizes his mistake, Thor will have Mjollnir back."

The gods dressed up Thor in a long wedding gown with a thick veil to hide his face and beard. His goats were rounded up and harnessed to his chariot, then they raced off through a gap in the sky.

When Thor and Loki reached Thrym's hall, a great wedding feast had begun. Thrym showed Thor to a throne at the head of the table and sat beside him on another. "Help yourself to food and drink," he said.

As always, Thor was starving. In a flash, he devoured a whole ox, followed by eight whole salmon. Thrym had never seen anyone eat so much. Quickly, Loki explained that "Freyja" was so excited about her wedding that she had not eaten for a week.

Delighted, Thrym called for Mjollnir to be brought forward to bless the bride. But, as soon as Mjollnir was within Thor's grasp, he snatched it and ripped off his veil. Then he raised the hammer and killed Thrym with a crushing blow.

MORE GODS AND GODDESSES

The Norse god of the sea was Njord. Originally one of the Vanir, he was handed over to the Aesir as a hostage after the war between the gods. Njord lived in a hall by the sea and ruled the wind and waves, bringing good luck to sailors and fishermen.

Njord married Skadi, the daughter of a giant called Thiazi, whom the gods had killed. As compensation for her father's death, she was allowed to pick one of the gods as her husband. Skadi chose Njord but their marriage was not a success. Skadi loved being in the mountains, whereas Njord could not live anywhere but the sea.

Did you know?

Njord was very important to the Norsemen because the sea played a vital part in their lives. Great seafarers, they built warships and merchant ships for raiding and trading far and wide. Their most famous ships were longships, warships that were strong enough to withstand the stormiest seas but light enough to be carried overland.

Apart from her chariot, Freyja also had a magic falcon skin. When she put it on, it gave her the power of flight.

FREYJA AND FREYR

Freyja and her brother, Freyr, were Njord's daughter and son. Freyja was goddess of love, beauty, and fertility, bringing good harvests and caring for pregnant women. She was also goddess of death, flying over the battlefield in a chariot pulled by two giant cats. Freyr was a fertility god who protected warriors in battle. His chariot was pulled by a golden boar that could run faster than the wind.

QUESTS AND ADVENTURES

Many characters in Norse myths went on great quests and adventures. One of them was Odin, king of the gods, who was also god of war and death. From his great throne in Asgard, Odin watched over the Nine Worlds. He was helped in this by two ravens that gathered news from around the Worlds, then perched on Odin's shoulders and whispered in his ears. Odin was married to Frigg, queen of the gods. Although he was stern and forbidding, he was also god of wisdom and poetry.

WHO'S WHO?

One of Odin's sons was Tyr, god of battle and law and order. The bravest god, he inspired warriors with courage in battle. Tyr is usually shown as a man with only one hand. The other hand was bitten off by a terrifying wolf, Fenrir (see page 34).

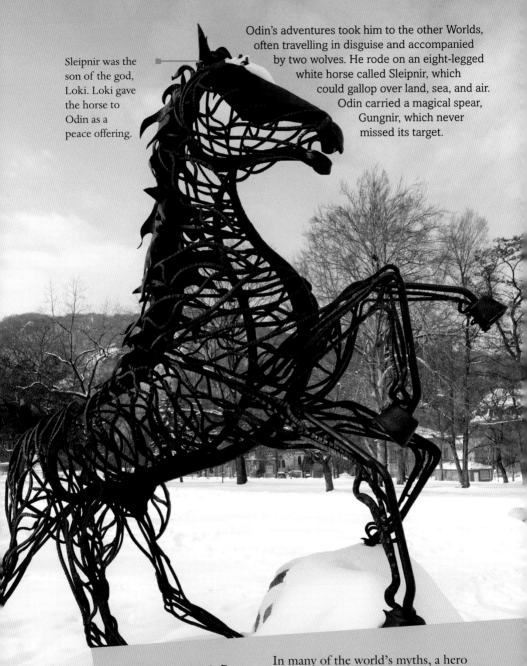

Sleipnir was the son of the god, Loki. Loki gave the horse to Odin as a peace offering.

Odin's adventures took him to the other Worlds, often travelling in disguise and accompanied by two wolves. He rode on an eight-legged white horse called Sleipnir, which could gallop over land, sea, and air. Odin carried a magical spear, Gungnir, which never missed its target.

MYTH LINKS

In many of the world's myths, a hero or god undertakes a quest that tests his courage or strength to the limits. In Greek mythology, for example, the hero, Hercules, has to complete 12 seemingly impossible tasks, or labours, to make amends for the deaths of his wife and children.

Odin and the mead of poetry

When the war between them ended, the gods all spat into a huge jar to seal the peace. From this spit, they shaped a man called Kvasir. He became famous for his great wisdom.

Two evil dwarves invited Kvasir to a feast where they killed him and mixed his blood with honey to make into mead. Whoever drank the mead would become a wise man or a poet. For years, the dwarves kept it a secret. Much later, they were forced to hand it over to a giant called Suttung. Suttung hid the mead deep in a cave under a mountain and set his beautiful daughter, Gunnlod, to guard it.

Before long, however, news of the magical mead reached the gods. "I will travel to the land of the giants to find it," vowed Odin.

Disguised as a giant, Odin made his way to a farm that was owned by Suttung's brother, Baugi. Odin tricked the farm workers into killing each other. Then he went to see Baugi. "I can tend your farm," he offered. "A giant like me can easily do the work of nine men."

"How much would I have to pay you?" asked Baugi.

"Not much," said Odin slyly. "Just a tiny sip of Suttung's mead."

"Never!" Suttung roared, when Baugi asked him.

"Then," Odin told Baugi, "you can help me find the mead for myself."

Baugi led Odin to the mountain and bored a deep hole with his magic drill. Odin turned himself into a snake, slithered through the hole, and turned back into himself again. As soon as Gunnlod saw him, she fell madly in love with him. She agreed to let him have just one sip of the mead but before she could stop him, he picked up the cauldron and drained the lot. Then, keeping the mead safely in his mouth, Odin turned into an eagle and sped back to Asgard.

POEMS AND RUNES

According to Norse mythology, Odin occasionally allowed humans a sip of the mead of poetry and they became poets, or skalds. In Norse society, skalds were highly respected and valued. They were hired to entertain chiefs and their guests at feasts, where they recited long and stirring poems about great kings, warriors, and battles.

WHO'S WHO?

Egill Skallagrimsson (c. 910–990) was one of the greatest Norse skalds. Born in Iceland, he composed his first work at the age of three. Years later, Egill was captured by his enemy, Eric Bloodaxe, king of Northumbria, and sentenced to death. He saved himself by reciting a dazzling poem in praise of the king.

THE QUEST FOR THE RUNES

The Norsemen used an alphabet consisting of 16 characters, called runes. These were written in straight lines so that they could be carved easily on to wood or stone. The Norsemen believed that the runes had magical powers which protected people from harm.

According to Norse mythology, Odin brought back the runes from the Land of the Dead in his quest for knowledge. To learn the runes, Odin put himself in great danger. He hung from the trunk of Yggdrasill, the World Tree, for nine days and nights, his body pierced by spears and without any food or drink. When he finally fell from the tree, alive, he was clutching the runes and their secret knowledge in his hands.

Norse runes were designed to be carved on to stone. Runestones like this one were often put up in memory of dead warriors.

WAR AND WARRIORS

As god of battle, Odin was said to cause wars on Earth by flinging down his spear. War was very important to the Norsemen and Norse warriors were greatly feared. Local chiefs kept bands of warriors for protection and to take part in raids. They were trained to fight with various weapons: spears, axes and, most importantly, swords. Warriors gave their swords fierce-sounding names, such as Leg-Biter and Adder, and were often buried alongside them.

THE HALL OF THE SLAIN

Dying in battle was the highest honour in Norse society. Only then could a warrior hope to enter Valhalla, the Hall of the Slain, Odin's magnificent home in Asgard. Valhalla had golden spears for walls, a roof thatched with golden shields, and 540 doors. Here, the warriors fought and feasted in preparation for the final battle of Ragnarok (see page 41). It was said that when the battle began, 800 warriors would march out of each door.

Norse warriors learned to fight and use weapons from a young age so that they were ready to join a raiding party.

Valkyrie

Did you know?

Freyja also had a hall for slain warriors. Half of the warriors killed in battle came to live in her hall, which was called Sessrumnir.

WHO'S WHO?

The Valkyries, or Choosers of the Slain, were beautiful female warriors who worked as Odin's messengers and servants. Riding on horses, they swooped over battlefields, choosing the bravest warriors of those killed to escort back to Valhalla. Their other duties included serving food and drink to the warriors in Valhalla.

CREATURES AND MONSTERS

Giants played a large part in Norse mythology. They were generally seen as evil creatures, determined to disrupt the world. They were constantly at war with the gods, even though many gods were related to giants by marriage. It was said that the giants would finally defeat the gods at Ragnarok.

A giant called Hrungnir once challenged Odin to a horse race. He chased Odin back to Asgard where he began boasting about killing the gods. The gods called on Thor for help. Thor hurled his hammer at the giant who was armed with a giant whetstone. Mjollnir broke the whetstone in two and struck Hrungnir on the head. The giant fell down dead on top of Thor. Despite their best efforts, the gods could not shift Hrungnir and, to their shame, had to call on Thor's young son for help.

DWARVES

Dwarves were mythical beings who lived in caves deep under mountains. According to Norse myth, the gods formed the dwarves from maggots that crawled out from Ymir's flesh (see pages 10–11). Though greedy and cunning, the dwarves were also highly skilled craftsmen, making magical objects out of gold, including the treasures of the gods.

Suttung was the giant who hid the mead of poetry from the gods until Odin stole it from him (see pages 24–25).

The dwarves made treasures for the gods, including Odin, shown here in disguise, and tried to win the gods' favour.

WHO'S WHO?

The dwarf Andvari lived underneath a waterfall. He could change into a fish at will and had a magical ring that had helped to make him rich. One day, Loki caught Andvari and stole his gold and ring. Andvari cursed them both to bring misery to whoever owned them.

Sigurd slays the dragon

Long ago, a man called Fafnir killed his father and stole his huge hoard of gold. This gold had once belonged to the dwarf, Andvari, and it was cursed. The curse would cause the death of its owner, but Fafnir did not care. As his greed for gold grew, he turned himself into a dragon, so he would be better able to guard his trove.

Meanwhile, Fafnir's brother Regin brought up their nephew, Sigurd, as his own son. Regin forged a powerful sword for Sigurd and the two set off to kill the dragon and bring back the gold.

Sigurd and Regin knew that they would need all of their cunning to defeat the dragon. First, Sigurd dug a trench across the path that Fafnir followed down to the stream where he went to drink.

"Wait in the trench, Sigurd," instructed Regin. "When Fafnir gets thirsty, he will crawl across, and you can kill him."

The ground soon began to shake as Fafnir came crawling down the path. In a flash, Sigurd drew out his sword and thrust it into Fafnir's body. The dragon was dead.

"Roast Fafnir's heart over the fire," Regin ordered. "I want to eat it."

Sigurd did as he was told, and to test if the heart was cooked, he poked it with his finger. The heart was hot and scalded him, so he sucked his finger to cool it down. As he did so, he swallowed some of the dragon's blood, and suddenly found that he could understand the speech of the birds twittering in the tree above him.

"There lies Regin," said one of the birds, "plotting to betray Sigurd and kill him so that he can have all of the gold for himself."

On hearing this, Sigurd drew his sword and cut off Regin's head. Then, taking a ring from the treasure trove, he set off on his travels and became the hero of many adventures.

MYTHICAL BEASTS

Many other monstrous and mythical beasts feature in Norse mythology. Jormungand was a gigantic serpent and the son of Loki. After warning that Jormungand would bring danger to the gods, Odin threw him into the sea. There, he grew so big that he could coil right around Earth and grasp his own tail in his mouth. His arch-enemy was Thor. It was foretold that the two would meet at Ragnarok when Thor would kill Jormungand, only to die shortly afterwards from the serpent's poison.

MONSTROUS WOLF

Another of Loki's terrible children was Fenrir, a gigantic wolf who grew so vicious and strong that the gods had to find a way of restraining him. They asked him to test his strength by being tied up with a magic rope, designed by the dwarves. Sensing a trick, Fenrir agreed but only if one of the gods put his hand in the wolf's mouth. Tyr volunteered and the gods tied Fenrir up. The harder the wolf struggled, the tighter the rope became, until he was so furious he bit Tyr's hand clean off. The gods imprisoned Fenrir underground.

Jormungand was once hooked by Thor on a fishing trip and struck on the head with Mjollnir. He always bore a grudge against Thor.

Did you know?

The magic rope used to bind Fenrir was made of "impossible things", such as the sound of a cat's footstep and the beard of a woman.

Thor went forth against Jö...

MYTH LINKS

Brave dragon-slayers appear in myths and legends from around the world. One of the most famous is St George. Legend tells how he killed a fierce dragon that was terrorising a town in the Middle East. He rescued the king's daughter whom the beast was about to eat.

THE END OF THE WORLD

The god Loki, who was the son of two giants, had a special place in Norse mythology. Loki's love of tricks, disguises, and adventures frequently got him, and the other gods, into trouble, though he was usually able to talk himself out of a fix. However, Loki could also be sly and cunning. As time went on, his tricks became more spiteful and the gods became more distrustful of his evil nature.

MYTH LINKS

Tricksters feature in many myths and legends, such as Coyote from Native American myth. Famous for his scheming, he is also able to change shape so that he can travel between the worlds of the humans and gods. His character reflects that of real-life coyotes, who are known for their intelligence and cunning.

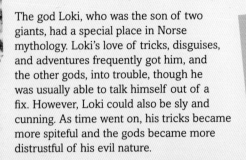

The coyote is a wild dog, found in North and Central America. Cunning and clever, they often appear in the region's myths.

LOKI AND THE APPLES

To get himself out of trouble, Loki once tricked the goddess Idunn into giving up the golden apples that kept the gods young. Loki persuaded her to leave Asgard with the apples, then she was snatched and carried away by a giant disguised as an eagle. The gods began to grow old and soon realized that Loki was to blame. Disguised as a falcon, Loki flew off and found Idunn in the giant's home. Quickly, he turned her into a nut and carried her back to Asgard in his beak. The gods killed the giant.

This stone has the face of the god Loki carved on it. ▪

Did you know?

The giant who carried off Idunn was Thiazi, father of Skadi. As compensation for his death, Skadi got to choose a god to be her husband.

The death of Balder

Wise and gentle Balder, the son of Odin and Frigg, had terrifying dreams about death. To make matters worse, there was a prophecy that he would be killed.

Frigg made everything in the Nine Worlds swear not to harm Balder. The gods turned this into a game. They hurled sticks, stones, and spears at Balder but it was impossible to hurt him.

Only Loki was not happy. He was jealous of Balder, and hatched a plan to get rid of him. Disguised as an old woman, he visited Frigg.

"Is it true that nothing can harm Balder?" she wheezed.

"Nothing," confirmed Frigg, "except mistletoe."

At once, Loki went to find some mistletoe. He sharpened one end of a sprig to make a dart. Then he found Balder's blind brother, Hod, who wanted to join in the gods' game.

"I'll tell you where Balder's standing," Loki said. "Here's a nice, sharp dart."

Hod grasped the dart and fired it at Balder. It struck him in the heart and he fell down dead. A stunned silence fell over Asgard. Finally, Frigg spoke.

"Who will travel to Hel?" she asked. "To bring Balder back from the dead?"

"I will," said Hermod, Balder's brother, and galloped off.

The gods gave Balder a hero's burial. They carried his body to the sea and placed it on a great ship, piled high with treasure. They set the ship alight and pushed it out to sea.

In Niflheim, Hermod pleaded with Hel to bring Balder back to life.

"If every single thing in the Nine Worlds mourns for him, he can return," she said. "But if even one thing does not weep, he must stay here for ever."

The gods sent messengers to every corner of the Nine Worlds, asking them to mourn for Balder. And everything began to weep … except one evil giantess.

So, Balder remained in the Land of the Dead, and the giantess, who was actually Loki in disguise, was overjoyed.

LOKI'S PUNISHMENT

After Balder's death, Loki's behaviour grew worse, until the gods decided that he must be punished. Loki tried to escape his fate by turning into a salmon. However, the gods caught him in a net and tied him across three rocks deep inside a dark mountain cave.

From the roof, the gods hung a huge snake that dripped poison onto Loki's face. Loki's faithful wife, Sigyn, stayed with him, catching the drops in a bowl. When she turned away to empty the bowl, the dreadful poison struck Loki, leaving him in agony.

It was foretold that Loki would break free of his chains and fight the gods at Ragnarok.

THE LAST BATTLE

According to a prophecy, Loki will eventually break free at Ragnarok, the great battle that will mark the end of the world and the doom of the gods. He and his evil children – Fenrir, Jormungand, and Hel – will attack Asgard, helped by the giants. The Nine Worlds will be destroyed, along with most of the gods and humans. All hope for the future is not lost, however. Yggdrasill will survive, along with a man and woman hiding among its branches. They will begin a new race of humans.

A new world will be born after Ragnarok.

Did you know?

Voluspa is the greatest poem of the *Poetic Edda* (see page 4). It is written as a prophecy, spoken by a prophetess to the god, Odin. It tells the story of the creation of the world and of the final battle that will destroy the gods and Earth. It is one of the most important sources of Norse mythology.

CHARACTERS, CREATURES, AND PLACES

Look at the words in brackets to find out how to say these Norse names.

GODS AND GODDESSES

Aesir (A-seer) group of Norse warrior gods that lived in Asgard, including Odin, Thor, Balder, and Frigg

Balder (Bal-der) popular Aesir god and son of Odin and Frigg

Freyja (Fray-ah) Vanir goddess of love, beauty, and fertility; daughter of Njord and sister of Freyr; owned a magic falcon skin that allowed her to fly

Freyr (Fray-er) fertility god who protected warriors in battle; son of Njord and brother of Freyja; married to Gerd, a giantess

Frigg (Frig) Queen of the gods; wife of Odin and mother of Balder and Bragi; visits Midgard in disguise to intervene in human lives

Heimdall (Hame-dall) Vanir god; guardian of Bifrost because of his super-sharp senses of sight and hearing

Hel (Hell) daughter of Loki; monstrous being, half alive, half dead, who rules over the Land of the Dead

Idunn (Id-doon) Aesir goddess; wife of Bragi

Loki (Lo-kee) mischief-making god; son of two giants and father of Jormungand, Fenrir, and Hel

Njord (Ny-ord) Vanir god and god of the sea; father of Freyja and Freyr; married to the giantess, Skadi

Odin (Oh-din) King of the gods; god of war, battle, and poetry; married to Frigg; all-seeing and all-powerful

Sif (Siff) goddess of harvest and plenty; married to Thor

Sigyn (Sig-in) goddess and wife of Loki; faithful and loving, despite his wicked behaviour

Thor (Thaw) Aesir god; great warrior, thunder god, and god of law and order; son of Odin and husband of Sif; defender of Asgard and arch-enemy of the giants

Tyr (Tewr) god of war; son of Odin

Vanir (Vah-neer) group of Norse gods; fertility gods including Njord, Freyja, Freyr, and Heimdall

GIANTS, DWARVES, AND OTHER CHARACTERS

Andvari (And-vari) dwarf who was forced to give his treasure to Loki but cursed it so that it brought death and misery to whoever owned it

Fafnir (Fahf-near) human who came into possession of Andvari's cursed gold; brother of Regin

Hrungnir (Hroong-near) giant who challenged Odin to a horse race and was killed in a duel by Thor

Regin (Ray-ghin) human and brother of Fafnir; brought up his nephew, Sigurd, to kill Fafnir and seize his gold; killed by Sigurd

Sigurd (Sig-urd) human and nephew of Fafnir and Regin; killed Fafnir and took his cursed gold; fell in love with the Valkyrie, Brynhild

Skadi (Skah-dee) giantess; daughter of Thiazi and married to Njord

Thiazi (Thyah-zee) giant; father of Skadi

Thrym (Thrim) giant who stole Thor's hammer, Mjollnir, and paid for it with his life

Valkyries (Val-kye-reez) female warriors who served Odin and chose the bravest warriors killed in battle to go to Valhalla

Ymir (Im-meer) first frost giant who was killed by Odin; his body formed Earth

PLACES

Asgard (Ass-gard) home of the Aesir gods

Bifrost (Bee-frost) Rainbow bridge between Asgard and Midgard

Ginnungagap (Ghin-un-ga-gap) great expanse of emptiness that existed between Muspell and Niflheim before the world was created

Jotunheim (Yot-oon-hame) mountainous land that is home to the giants

Midgard (Mid-gard) home of humans

Muspell (Moo-spell) land of fire, guarded by the fire giant, Surt

Niflheim (Niffle-hame) land of ice and darkness; location of Hel (Land of the Dead)

Valhalla (Val-hal-ah) Odin's hall in Asgard, where dead warriors feasted, fought, and prepared for Ragnarok

Vanaheim (Van-ah-hame) home of the Vanir gods

Yggdrasill (Igg-dra-sill) world tree; giant ash tree that held up the Nine Worlds

CREATURES

Fenrir (Fen-rear) monstrous wolf; son of Loki

Garm (Garm) huge dog that guards the entrance to Niflheim; ferocious, with a blood-stained chest

Jormungand (Yore-mun-gand) gigantic serpent; son of Loki

Sleipnir (Slape-neer) magical, eight-legged horse that belonged to Odin

GLOSSARY

chariot vehicle with two or four wheels that is pulled by a horse or other animal

compensation something given to make up for a loss, injury, or death

converted changed from one religion or set of beliefs to another

coyote animal similar to a dog or wolf that lives in the deserts and prairies of North America

dwarf in Norse myth, supernatural being created from maggots crawling on the body of the giant, Ymir. Dwarves are skilled craftsmen who live under the ground.

fertile able to produce new life, new plants, or animals

fertility ability to produce new life, new plants, or animals

forged when metal is heated and hammered to make weapons and tools

giant in Norse myth, supernatural being who is the enemy of the gods. Giants are enormously strong and able to change shape.

glacier huge river of ice that flows down mountains into the sea

guardian someone who looks after, protects, or defends a place

Hindu relating to the Hindu religion, which began in India more than 4,000 years ago

hostage person held as security to make sure that a promise is kept

immortal living forever; describes a being who cannot be killed

lava red-hot, liquid rock that bursts from the ground when a volcano erupts

maize plant that is also known as sweetcorn

mead strong drink made using honey

mistletoe plant with waxy white berries that often grows on oak trees

Mjollnir (Myoll-neer) Thor's hammer which was made by the dwarves

prophecy prediction of what will happen in the future

prophetess woman who makes a prophecy

prose spoken or written language that is not poetical

quest long, difficult search for something

Ragnarok (Rag-na-rock) great battle between the gods and giants at the end of the world

rune character in the Norse alphabet

sacrificed killed and offered to the gods to earn their favour or goodwill

skald professional poet in Norse society

source place where information comes from. This may be a person, an object, or a book.

supernatural describes beings or events that cannot be explained by natural or scientific laws

trickster character in myths who plays tricks and makes mischief

truce agreement to stop fighting during a war

whetstone stone used for sharpening knives and other tools

FIND OUT MORE

BOOKS

10 Best Viking Legends Ever, Michael Cox (Scholastic, 2009)

The Vikings (All About Ancient Peoples), Anita Ganeri
(Franklin Watts, 2009)

Vicious Vikings (Horrible History), Terry Deary (Scholastic, 2007)

Viking Blood: A Viking Warrior AD 1008 (My Story), Andrew Donkin
(Scholastic, 2008)

WEBSITES

www.bbc.co.uk/history/ancient/vikings
This website investigates the lives of the Vikings (Norsemen) and
the evidence for what we know about their culture.

www.bbc.co.uk/history/handsonhistory/vikings.shtml
A humorous, animated website about the Vikings, which allows you
to step back in time to AD 876 and make your own Viking longship.

www.bbc.co.uk/cbbc/shows/horrible-histories
This website of the hit TV series has a Viking game to play. Help to
guide some Vikings on an expedition and them on their quest.

PLACES TO VISIT

Jorvik Viking Centre
Coppergate
York YO1 9WT
www.jorvik-viking-centre.co.uk
The Jorvik Viking Centre stands on the site of a 1,000-year-old
Viking settlement, excavated in the city of York. Travel around the
site to experience what it was like to live in a Viking town.

The British Museum
Great Russell Street
London WC1B
www.britishmuseum.org
Visit the Viking gallery at the British Museum in London to see
artefacts such as coins and jewellery.

The Viking Ship Museum
Huk Aveny 35
0287 Oslo
Norway
www.khm.uio.no/vikingskipshuset/index_eng.html
This amazing museum houses several complete or nearly
complete Viking longships and many other artefacts.

The Viking Ship Museum
Vindeboder 12
DK-4000 Roskilde
Denmark
www.vikingeskibsmuseet.dk/en
Visit the museum to see five reconstructed Viking ships, and get
the chance to go sailing in a longship, as well as find out how the
ships were built.

FURTHER RESEARCH
Which Norse myth did you like reading most in this book? Which
characters did you find most interesting? Can you find out about
any more myths in which these characters appear? You could look
in the books or on the websites given on page 46, or even visit
some of the places mentioned above. You could also try retelling
your favourite myth in new way, such as in a diary, a cartoon strip,
or a newspaper report.

INDEX